카운트다운
Countdown

지성.감성의 메타언어
조선문학사시인선.949

카운트다운
Countdown

이원로 시집
The Poetry Collection of Lee Won-Ro

조선문학사

Contents 차례

Prologue 프롤로그
Countdown 카운트다운 ·················· 10

Part I 제1부
Triumph 개선

Triumph 개선 ·························· 14
The primal Vitality 원초의 생기 ·········· 16
A Speck of Dust 티끌 ·················· 18
Embrace 포옹 ·························· 20
Early Autumn 초가을 ·················· 22
Red Clay Path 황톳길 ·················· 24
Ebb and Flow 밀물 썰물 ················ 26
Crumbs 부스러기 ······················ 28
Orbit of Temptation 마의 궤도 ·········· 30
Palm Sunday 종려주일 ················ 32
Sight 시각 ···························· 34

Part II 제2부

Climax 절정

Climax 절정	38
Vanguard 선봉장	40
Time and Place 때와 장소	42
Changed Mimicrye 달라진 흉내	44
The Experience 체험	46
Easter 2024 부활절 2024	48
A Glimpse of Tomorrow 내일 예습	50
Writing 글쓰기	52
Fresh Verdure 신록	54
Stepping Stones 징검다리	56
Across the Divide 건너편	58

Part III 제3부
Annular Eclipse 금환식

Annular Eclipse 금환식 ········· 62
Rust and Moss 녹과 이끼 ········· 64
Winter Vaccination 겨울 접종 ········· 66
Protective Membrane 보호막 ········· 68
The Endless Ladder 끝없는 사다리 ········· 70
Poor Tree 가여운 나무 ········· 72
Color Is Light 색이 빛이지 ········· 74
Ostrich 타조 ········· 76
Beyond the River 강 저편 ········· 78
Reality and Illusion 실상과 허상 ········· 80
Face to Face 대면 ········· 82

Part IV 제4부
Digger 캐내는 사람

Stadium 경기장 ·································· 86
Passage Rite 통과의식 ······················ 88
Digger 캐내는 사람 ···························· 90
Predestined Days 정해진 나날 ··········· 92
Seasonal Light 계절의 빛 ··················· 94
The Sound of Knocking 두드리는 소리 ········ 96
My own Time 나만의 시간 ················· 98
Disappointment 실망 ·························· 100
Entrance and Exit 입구와 출구 ··········· 102
Execution 처형 ···································· 104
Solitary Egret 해오라기 ······················ 106

Part V 제5부
Possible and Impossible 가능과 불가능

Waves 파도 ……………………………………… 110
Impregnable Fortress 철옹성 …………………… 112
Wind and Door 바람과 문 ……………………… 114
Yoga Walk 요가 산책 …………………………… 116
Warning Signs 경고신호 ………………………… 118
Possible and Impossible 가능과 불가능 ………… 120
Empty House 빈집 ……………………………… 122
Bystander 방관자 ………………………………… 124
Spring Vibes 봄기운 ……………………………… 126
Flames 불꽃 ……………………………………… 128
Buds 새싹 ………………………………………… 130

Epilogue 에필로그

Perspective 원근법 ················· 132

About the Author 글쓴이 ················· 134

❚ Prologue ❚

Countdown

The countdown is indeed
The moment of truth.

If we pass
The final inspection,

We will seize the opportunity
For amazing joy.

We will rise up to
Another different tomorrow.

Everyone in the world
Lives in the middle of this.

| 프롤로그 |

카운트다운

초읽기는 실로
진실의 순간

최종 점검을
넘게 된다면

놀라운 환희의
기회를 만끽하리

또 다른 내일로
솟아오르지

세상 모두는
이 가운데 살지

제 1 부
개선

Part I
Triumph

Triumph

Even when the trumpets of triumph
blare across the sky,
Earthquakes erupt lava.

Across the battlefield strewn with corpses,
Where defeated soldiers flee,
The sky remains clear and blindingly blue.

In the eyes that gaze upward,
The river always flows serenely,
And the kite soars high.

Who is the victor of today?
Who is the victor of the century?
Who is the victor of eternity?

개선

개선의 행진 나팔이
하늘에 울려 퍼지는 날에도
지진은 용암을 분출하지

패잔병이 도망쳐 가는
시체 깔린 산야에도
하늘은 푸르고 눈부시리

머리 들어 바라보는 눈엔
강은 언제나 유유히 흐르지
솔개는 높이 솟아오르지

누가 오늘의 개선장군이지
누가 세기의 개선장군이지
누가 영원의 개선장군이지

The Primal Vitality

Buds and leaves
Will sprout astonishingly,
Will shine dazzlingly.

Into bodies, minds, and souls,
Exhausted and gasping
From last night's nightmares,
The primal vitality will be poured.

Bright colors
Carried by fresh winds
Will sweep away the darkness cleanly.

A seed, deeply planted,
A very long time ago,
Having overcome the cold and dark night,
Will finally bloom in colors of wonder.

원초의 생기

놀랍게 돋아나리
눈부시게 빛나리
꽃봉오리 잎망울들

어젯밤 흉몽에
허덕이며 지친
몸과 마음과 영혼에
원초의 생기가 부어지리

화창한 빛깔이
신선한 바람에 실려
어둠을 말끔히 밀어내리

아주 오래오래 전
깊이 넣어준 씨가
춥고 어두운 밤 이기고 드디어
경이의 빛깔로 피어나지

A Speck of Dust

A fleeting moment of glory,
A mere speck of dust,
We, travelers, passing through
This world of splendor and dust.

Though we know it well,
With all our heart and soul,
We struggle our whole lives to grasp it.
Are we obsessed with it because we're mortal?
It must be driven by our survival instinct.

It must be a deep-seated desire
To catch even a speck of dust.
Even if it's only for a moment of glory,
We're eager to grasp and fly away with it.

티끌

찰나의 영화이지
날아가는 티끌이지
영화와 티끌 세상을
스쳐 가는 나그네들

잘 알고 있으련만
몸과 마음 뜻을 다해
잡으려 평생 발버둥 치지
사라지기에 집착하는지
심어 넣어준 생존본능이지

티끌이라도 잡고 싶은
깊이 도사린 갈망이겠지
찰나의 영화라도 끝내
잡아들고 날려 가려 서리

Embrace

Opening your chest to your heart's content,
Do you want to embrace the blowing wind?
Taking a deep breath in,
Do you try to hold everything within?

The melody of flower rain dancing in the wind,
The spectacle of a blizzard enveloping the world,
The revelation of a falling meteor shower
And countless myths and whispers within.

Astonishingly beautiful,
You long to be one with them.
Drawn by an irresistible pull,
You spread the arms wide and embrace them.

Something must have drawn you here.
It was so surprising and beautiful
That you are inhaling deeply
And try to suck everything in it.

포옹

가슴을 마음껏 벌려
불어오는 바람을 안으려나
숨을 크게 깊이 들이마셔
모두를 안에 담아 넣으려나

바람에 날리는 꽃비의 선율
천지를 뒤덮는 눈보라의 장관
쏟아져 내리는 유성우의 묵시
그 안의 무수한 신화와 속삭임

놀랍게 아름다워
함께 하나 되고 싶으리
거역할 수 없는 끌림에
크게 팔 벌려 끌어안으리

무언가에 끌려 나왔으리
너무나 놀랍고 아름다워
숨을 깊이 크게 들이마셔
그 안의 모두를 빨아들이지

Early Autumn

Early autumn is truly
A time of no small toil.
After the drenching monsoon,
We must raise and trim the fruit trees,
Cleaning the fruits covered in mud,
And tending to them diligently.

Still, all this,
Nurturing and growing,
Ripening and harvesting,
It's all worth it.

From now on, all things
Will be on our side.
Brightness fills the heavens and earth.
We shall welcome the harvest of joy.
Even hopes trapped in dark clouds
Will become brighter and stronger.

초가을

초가을은 진정
쉽지 않은 때리
장마에 쏠렸던
과수를 세워 다듬고
흙탕물에 덮친 열매를
씻어주고 공들여야지

그래도 이만치
맺어주고 키워주고
익혀주고 여물게 하니
이게 다 얼만가

이제부턴 모두가
우리 편이 될 거야
천지에 빛이 찬란해
기쁨의 추수를 맞이하리
먹구름에 갇혔던 소망도
더욱 뚜렷하고 단단해지리

Red Clay Path

Treading on the red clay path, they say,
One can attain longevity and well-being,
So everyone competes to fill the path.

Above the trees,
Towering high on either side of the path,
The dazzling sky smiles.

The expression of the watchtower,
Holding the key, looking down from above,
Is hard to decipher.

As they tread down the red clay path,
They wish for their desires to be fulfilled,
With each step, they solidify their conviction.

황톳길

황톳길을 밟아 다지면
만수무강을 한다기에
모두 다투어 길이 메지

높이 치솟아 늘어선
길 양쪽 나무들 위에
눈부신 하늘이 미소 짓는다

열쇠를 쥐고 위에서
내려다보는 망루의 표정
읽기가 쉽지 않으리

황톳길을 다지면서
소원성취를 간구하리
발짝마다 확신을 다져가리

Ebb and Flow

The waves and foam
Emerge with the incoming tide,
And break with the outgoing tide.

I can't help but feel
Sorry for their
Trials and tribulations.
I offer my entreaty.

However, they are cute and heartwarming
With curiosity and joy,
Every minute and every second.

Feeling and thoughts,
Carried by the flow and
Pushed away by the ebb.

밀물 썰물

밀물에 생겨나
썰물에 부서지는
파도와 거품들

나는 그들의
시련과 고난이
못내 안타까워
탄원을 올리지

하나 그들은 일분일초
호기심과 기쁨으로
아기자기하단다
가슴 뿌듯하단다

밀물에 실려와
썰물에 밀려가는
느낌과 생각들

Crumbs

Like something that will be swept away,
Insignificant crumbs
Hold up the world,
And keep it from withering away.

A crumb of compassion,
A crumb of comfort,
A crumb of nobility,
A crumb of justice.

They fill in the broken gaps,
They connect the broken pieces.
They wrap up the wounds and heal them.
They bring the joy of revival.

The insignificant crumbs
Pile up and up,
And one day, surprisingly,
They will rise up to touch the sky.

부스러기

불려 사라질 것 같은
하찮은 부스러기가
세상을 붙들어 세우고
시들어 죽지 않게 하지

연민 부스러기
위로 부스러기
고결 부스러기
정의 부스러기

깨진 틈새를 메우지
부러진 데를 이어주리
상처를 싸매 낫게 하지
소생의 기쁨을 안겨주리

보잘것없는 부스러기가
쌓이고 또 쌓여 오르며
언제인가는 놀랍게도
하늘에 닿게 솟아오르리

Orbit of Temptation

In the mesmerizing gaze,
The orbit of temptation always lies,
A stage where desire ignites.

Led by arrogance and greed,
One might find themselves trapped,
In the tunnel of madness.

The orbit of temptation, akin to
The main orbit, runs alongside,
Always ready to switch paths.

Even while orbiting the main track,
In a blink of an eye, one finds themselves
Drawn into the orbit of temptation.

마의 궤도

한눈파는 눈에는 언제나
마의 궤도는 매력적이지
군침이 도는 절호의 무대지

오만과 탐욕이 이끌어가는
광란의 터널에 갇히게 되리
환각과 공황의 도미노이지

마의 궤도는 본궤도와
같이 달리는 쌍둥이 궤도
언제라도 바꿔 탈 수 있지

본궤도를 돌면서도
한눈파는 순간 어느 사이
마의 궤도에 끌려가 있지

Palm Sunday

Though the sight remains the same,
Reactions are all different.
Cheers may echo, yet the meaning varies,
From pure faith to ulterior motives.

Selfless faith,
Self-denial obedience,
Is this an endless journey?
Isn't it an eternal homework?

With differing goals,
Perspectives shift,
Praise and curses follow
In swift succession.

They went crazy waving palm branches,
Laying down their garments in praise.
Yet days later, their hearts turned cold,
Crucifying the one they once hailed.

Does anyone really know
His true entirety?
Let alone in advance, we won't know
Even after the events have come to pass.

종려주일

똑같이 보는데
반응은 다르지
외침은 같으나
내용은 다르리

사심 없는 믿음
자기부정의 순종
끝없이 가는 길인지
영원한 숙제 아닌지

목적이 다르니
보는 게 다르리
덩달아 칭송하고
덩달아 저주하리

종려나무 가지 흔들며
겉옷을 깔아 열광하더니
며칠 후 돌연 변심해
십자가에 못 박았지

진정한 그의 모습
실로 아는 이 누군가
미리 알기는커녕
지난 다음도 모르리

Sight

What is scattering
And disappearing here is,
What is flowing in
And gathering there.

When your sight aligns right,
You will see the scheduled order,
Sadness and regret transform,
Becoming anticipation and joy.

The clutter will
Clear away like fog,
And the time of encounter
Silently approaches.

All things return to
Their proper stations,
Yet where have you
Built your nest?

시각

여기서는
흩어져 사라지는 게
저기서는
흘러와 모이는 것

시각이 제대로 잡히면
예정된 순서를 보게 되리
아쉬움도 서러움도
기다림과 기쁨이 되리

어수선하던 때가
안개처럼 걷혀가며
마주 서는 시간이
말없이 다가오리

모두 자리 대로
돌아가고 있는데
너는 어디에
둥지를 틀었는지

제 2 부
절정

Part II
Climax

Climax

Every climax is accompanied by
A trembling.

The climax of ecstasy,
The zenith of sorrow,
Like two faces of a supernova,
The apex of creation,
The peak of extinction.
Splendor and withering
Are always mixed together.

It's not only the climax that's the climax,
Every moment is a climax.

Even if we live within the apex,
We don't know because we are dull.
Throughout the macrocosm and microcosm,
The flames of every moment
Forge the chain of climax.
The acme of destruction
Is the apex of creation.

Every culmination is accompanied by
A resonance.

절정

모든 절정에는
떨림이 있지

환희의 절정
비애의 극치
초신성의 양면이지
생성의 정점
소멸의 극치이지
영화와 조락은
늘 함께 섞이지

절정만이 절정이 아니지
모든 순간이 절정이지

정점 안에 살며
무디기에 모르리
대 소우주 어디나
매 순간의 불꽃이
절정의 사슬을 이루리
소멸의 절정이
생성의 정점이지

모든 정점에는
울림이 있지

Vanguard

Carrying the burden of the world alone,
Navigating the path of the universe,
How long are you going to call yourself a brave
And peerless vanguard?

Are you always confident?
Are you anxious and worried everywhere?
Are you scared, but there's no way to avoid it?
Is there someone you can lean on?

In the eyes that only see the confrontation,
It's a dark valley of suffering and agony.
In the heart of conciliation,
The world will become wider and richer.

A new day dawns.
You have to go out into the world and face it.
Still everything,
Do you want to handle it alone?

선봉장

세상의 짐을 홀로 지고
우주의 길을 헤쳐가는
용맹 무쌍한 선봉자로
어느 때까지 자처하려나

언제나 자신만만인지
어디서나 노심초사인지
두려우나 피할 길 없어선가
누군가 믿는 데가 있어선가

대결만 보는 눈에는
고난과 고뇌의 골짜기이지
양보하는 마음에는
세상은 넓어지고 풍요하리

새날이 밝아오지
세상을 나가 맞아야지
아직도 모든 걸
홀로 감당하려느냐

Time and Place

Snow-covered branches,
Icicles on the shady place,
But water droplets on the sunny place.
Everything is as it's allowed to be.

I want to be snow,
But will I become snow?
I want to be ice,
But I won't become ice.

Snow and ice are both temporary,
Who knows when it will be water?
Who knows where it will become vapor?
It's all about time and place.

때와 장소

눈에 덮인 가지들
응달에는 고드름인데
양달에는 물방울이지
매사는 갖춰지는 대로리

눈이 되고 싶다고
눈이 되겠는지
얼음이 되고 싶어
얼음이 되지 않으리

눈도 얼음도 한때
언제 물로 될지
어디서 증기가 될지
모두가 때와 장소지

Changed Mimicry

The winter river meets the ally
And its pace becomes quite brisk.
Even the cold wind of the harsh winter
Is now a tailwind, since the path is the same.

The wind goes its own way,
The watercourse goes its own way,
They will raise the cry of march.
In a world addicted to games,
There is no distinction between ally and enemy.
One step ahead is the difference between life and death.

Amid all this noise and commotion,
What is it that is being newly established?
Looking deeply into each one,
It is only the mimicry that has changed.

달라진 흉내

겨울 강이 우군을 만나
걸음이 제법 잽싸 졌다
엄동설한의 찬바람도
길이 같으니 순풍이지

바람은 바람대로
물길은 물길대로
행군의 외침을 높이리
게임에 중독된 세상
우군 적군이 따로 없지
한발 먼저가 생과 사이지

그렇게 야단법석 떨며
새로 세우는 게 뭐 있지
하나하나 깊이 들여다보니
흉내가 달라졌을 뿐이네

The Experience

Even though it resides within us,
We must enter and experience it,
To truly understand heaven.

You entered and stayed there for a while,
How long was it?
Seconds, minutes, or hours?

How were you able to enter?
What is the secret
To staying longer?

How similar will
Your experience be to mine?
Is this experience the true heaven?

Everyone will
Eventually go there,
Why do we feel so restless?

체험

제 안에 살아도
들어가서 체험해야
진정 천국이지

그 안에 들어가
얼마간 머물렀지
몇 초 몇 분 몇 시간

어떻게 거기에
들어갈 수 있었지
오래 머무는 비결은

너와 나의 체험은
얼마나 같을지
이 체험이 그 천국일지

모두가 결국
그렇게 될 것인데
무얼 조바심치지

Easter 2024

It seemed like it was going
To bloom,, but it was hesitant.
It finally blossoms today.
This will bring glory on
The day of resurrection.

Is that possible?
Can it really be?
A miracle has happened,
This is truly the long-awaited day,
The joy of conviction blooms brightly.

Those who believe because they have seen,
Those who believe even without seeing,
Those who see and yet do not believe,
All will be embraced equally
In the light of glory.

Things that have budded,
Things in full bloom,
Flower petals flying away,
All are full of glorious light,
Under the beautiful sky.

부활절 2024

필 듯 피어날 듯
머뭇거리더니
오늘에야 활짝 피네
부활의 날에
영광을 올리려나

그럴 수 있을 건가
정말 그럴 건가 하더니
기적이 일어났지
진정 고대하던 날이지
확신의 기쁨이 활짝 피리

보았기에 믿는 이
안 보아도 믿는 이
보고도 안 믿는 이
모두에게 골고루
영광의 빛을 안겨주리

봉오리 진 것들
만개한 것들
날려가는 꽃잎들
아름다운 하늘 아래
모두 영광의 빛 가득하지

A Glimpse of Tomorrow

This fleeting moment, a mere brushstroke of time,
Is a rehearsal for the dawning of tomorrow.

Though unseen and unheard,
Do not dismiss its significance.

A lot of things that were overlooked
Are tomorrow put into today.

Now we finally realize the truth,
Regret gnawing at our hearts for lost time.

This is a fleeting moment, a mere brushstroke of time,
But within it lies the rehearsal for a glorious tomorrow.

The clouds will part, and light will shine through,
And all things will be made new.

내일 예습

지금은 잠시 스쳐 가는 순간
다가올 내일을 예습하는 때

안 보이고 안 들린다고
생 투정하지 마시게

간과해 버린 많은 것
오늘 안에 넣어준 내일이지

이제야 겨우 알아챘지
놓친 시간이 안타까우리

오늘은 스쳐 가는 순간이지
펼쳐질 내일을 예습하는 때

구름을 뚫고 빛이 새 나오리
만사가 다시 새로워지리

Writing

By following every command,
I have transcended the realm of instinct,
Stepping into the next phase of existence.

I have seen
what cannot be seen,
Heard
what cannot be heard,
Written
what cannot be spoken.

I have seen what I was told to see,
Heard what I was told to hear,
Written what I was told to write.

글쓰기

하라는 대로 했기에
본능의 차원을 넘어
다음에 들어섰으리

볼 수 없는걸
보았으리
들을 수 없는걸
들었으리
말로 할 수 없는걸
써냈으리

보라는 대로 보았으리
들으라는 대로 들었으리
쓰라는 대로 써냈으리

Fresh Verdure

The fresh verdure seeps
Into the back alleys of my heart
Where the flower petals
Have blown away.

As the stream always shows,
As the birds sing like that,
Where the first has passed,
The next always comes in.

Drawn to something,
The moment I look up,
The vibrant light green dazzles,
Astonishingly stirring my soul.

Faster than light,
The wings of imagination
Soar toward the source of verdure,
Beyond the horizon.

신록

꽃잎이 날려간
가슴의 뒤안길로
신록의 싱그러움이
스며들어 오네

냇물이 항시 보여주듯
새들이 그처럼 노래하듯
먼저가 스쳐 간 자리엔
언제나 다음이 들어서지

무언가에 마음이 끌려
눈 들어 바라보는 순간
발랄한 연초록 눈부심이
놀랍게 영혼을 울리지

빛보다 빠른
상상의 날개가
신록의 원천을 향해
지평 너머로 날아오르지

Stepping Stones

My dreams are soaked with worries,
I wake up in a daze,
The aftertaste lingers,
Heavy and bitter.

Will the sky fall
And the earth collapse?
Can anxiety alone
Solve anything?

No matter what anyone says,
No matter how dark and trembling you are,
There is tomorrow,
Not just now.

After all this, it will be nothing,
You'll blush with embarrassment and regret,
These are just the stepping stones
That lead you to the next path.

징검다리

꿈이 온통 걱정으로
뒤범벅이 되어버렸지
얼떨결에 깨어났어도
여운이 만만치 않으리

하늘이 내려앉고
땅이 꺼질 건가
노심초사만으로 어찌
해결될 문제이겠나

누가 뭐라 해도
어둡고 떨려도
지금만이 아니라
내일이 있지

지나고 나면 별것 아니리
무안하고 송구해 얼굴 붉히리
다음 길로 인도되어 가는
밟게 될 징검다리들이지

Across the Divide

I've just realized
That there's a front and a back.
I wonder when I'll ever fully grasp
The existence of the other side.

The wolf howls
At the sight of the moon.
The dog goes crazy
At the sight of a solar eclipse.

It's so shocking
That we might faint,
So he'll show us one by one
When the time is right.

건너편

앞과 뒤가 있는걸
이제 겨우 알았지
건너편이 있는 건
언제나 깨닫게 될지

늑대가 달을 보고
울부짖는다
개는 일식을 보고
혼비백산하지

너무나 놀라워
혼절하겠기에
때가 되어야
하나씩 보여주리

제 3 부
금환식

Part III
Annular Eclipse

Annular Eclipse

The world is abuzz
With the excitement of the annular eclipse.
We watch in hushed silence
As the Moon's shadow swallows the Sun
Like a ring being formed.
The eclipse observers are all ecstatic.

The celestial wonder that once terrified
Primitive humans
Shakes the souls of modern man.
The solar plasma bursts forth
Pushing aside the Moon's shadow.
Mystery and miracles
Have an undeniable power
Over everyone.

Every moment is a revelation,
Veiling and revealing,
Opening and revealing,
A truly ingenious design.
We watch the same wonder,
But it will be engraved differently in our hearts.

금환식

온 세상이 떠들썩하지
금환식 구경으로 법석이지
달그림자에 잠식되어가는
해 모습을 숨죽여 바라보리
약혼반지가 이뤄지는 순간
일식 관찰자 모두 열광하지

원시인을 질겁하게 하던
천상의 경이가 여지없이
현대인의 영혼을 흔들지
달그림자 비집고 드러나는
해 플라스마에 탄성이 터지지
신비와 기적은 누구에게나
뿌리칠 수 없는 위력이지

매 순간이 계시이지
가리면서 드러내 주고
열면서 드러내 주지
실로 오묘한 설계이지
같이 바라보는 경이지만
마음에는 달리 새겨지리

Rust and Moss

Still clinging
Torn, pushed until falling,
Tormented by nightmares.

Dust and specks
Of obsession, fear, and darkness
Cover all over the web of consciousness,
Making it hard to escape.

Though I long only for joyful dreams,
The rust and moss must first be cleared away
For the mind's net to function properly.

녹과 이끼

아직도 매달리고
차이고 밀려 떨어지는
흉몽에 시달린다지

집착과 두렴과 어둠의
먼지와 티끌이 온통
의식 망에 서려 있으니
벗어나기 쉽지 않으리

기쁜 꿈만을 간구하지만
녹과 이끼를 먼저 걷어내야
뇌 망이 제대로 작동하리

Winter Vaccination

Setting everything aside on the first day of November,
I will step out to receive the winter vaccination
To safely get through the season of mistletoe.

Making a fuss to not be carried away by illness,
I receive the preventive shot.

So that I do not give up, overwhelmed by snowstorms,
And do not lose my way in the dark,
This is the latest developed miraculous vaccine.

With the best troops around to protect,
The hardships of winter will surely ease.

겨울 접종

모두 제쳐놓고 11월 첫날
겨울 접종 받으러 나아가리
겨우살이를 무사히 해 달라지

잘못 걸려 날려가지 않게
예방주사 맞느라 법석 떨지

눈보라에 덮쳐 자포자기 안 하게
어둠에 걸려 길 잃지 않게 해줄
최신 개발된 신묘한 백신이지

최정예부대가 둘러 지켜 주려니
이해 겨우살이는 한시름 놓게 되리

Protective Membrane

Frequently, signals will be sent,
The eyes of temptation will often,
Deeply stir my heart.

I will be swept away by rapture,
If I slip once,
It will be a bottomless abyss.

At the moment I am about to be drawn in
By the dazzling appearance,
A sudden barrier appears.

It will prevent me from
Falling into the world of evil.
It will create a protective membrane.

Since it's a multifaceted world,
It won't be easy to discern
Who is putting up the barrier.

보호막

신호를 자주 보내리
유혹의 눈길이 자주
마음을 깊이 흔들리

황홀에 말려들리
한번 미끄러지면
밑 빠진 심연이지

경탄할 모습에
빨려 들어갈 찰나
난데없는 차단막

흉물의 세계로
빠져들지 않게
보호막을 쳐주리

많은 측면 세상이니
누가 내리는 막인지
구별이 쉽지 않으리

The Endless Ladder

I thought
This was all,
But it won't be.

I felt
This was the end,
But this isn't the end.

I thought
Now was the only chance,
But now isn't the only time.

I thought
That was all,
But that isn't all.

Self-contradiction,
My brain and me,
The endless ladder.

끝없는 사다리

이게 다인 줄
알았더니
그렇진 않으리

여기가 끝인 줄
느꼈더니
여기가 끝은 아니리

지금이 오직 기회라
생각했더니
지금이 유일은 아니지

그게 다인가
했더니
그게 다는 아니다

자가당착
뇌와 나
끝없는 사다리

Poor Tree

In the gentle breeze,
The tree surfs and plays,
But when the wind grows strong,
Its branches break and fall away,
And in a whirlwind's sway,
Its roots are torn from the soil.

Oh, poor trees,
The wind that once brought joy,
Now threatens to destroy,
And so they live in fear,
Unsure of what to do or how to steer,
They wonder who is sending the wind.

Already on life's stage they stand,
Happy yet sad,
Easy yet overwhelming,
Peaceful yet troubled,
A marvelous yet frightening
Scenario they must unravel.

가여운 나무

산들바람이 불면 나무는
바람을 서핑하며 놀리
바람이 세어지면
가지가 부러지지
바람이 소용돌이치면
뿌리까지 뽑히게 되리

가여운 나무들 한때
타고 놀게 준 바람인데
언제 마음이 돌변할지 몰라
전전긍긍하며 살아가리
어찌하려고 무얼 하라고
누가 보내는 바람인지

이미 무대에 올랐으니
기쁘나 서럽고
쉬운 듯 벅차고
평안한 듯 괴롭고
경이로우나 무서운
시나리오를 해내야지

Color Is Light

Light pours forth,
Color will burst forth.
Light is color,
Color is light.

Underneath the vivid autumn sky,
The colors are at their peak in the world.
They must have absorbed the light.

What if it turns into a monster?
Will it turn out the way you desire?
Leaves and blades of grass,
Only clinging to the promise, they must have run.

Color is not produced, but received,
They would have opened their hearts and let in the light.
I wonder what happened to the worried mind.

색이 빛이지

빛이 쏟아지지
색이 분출하리
빛이 색이고
색이 빛이지

가을이 완연한 하늘 아래
색깔이 산야에 절정이네
빛을 받아 물이 들었으리

흉물이 되면 어쩌니
바라는 대로 될 건지
나뭇잎들 풀잎들
약속만 붙들고 달렸으리

색은 내는 게 아니라 드는 거지
그들은 가슴을 열고 빛을 들였으리
걱정 근심하던 마음은 어찌 되었지

Ostrich

Without walking,
the ability to walk fades.
Without running,
the ability to run fades.
Without flying,
the ability to fly fades.
The stubborn ostrich.

Without seeing,
the ability to see fades.
Without listening,
the ability to hear fades.
Without embracing,
the ability to love fades.
The longing for the other side.

Without writing,
the ability to write fades.
Without drawing,
the ability to draw fades.
Without blowing,
the ability to blow fades.
The trumpet player.

타조

안 걸으면 못 걷게 되리
안 뛰면 못 뛰게 되리
안 날면 못 날게 되리
완강한 타조

안 보면 못 보게 되리
안 들으면 못 듣게 되리
안 품으면 못 품게 되리
피안의 동경

안 쓰면 못 쓰게 되리
안 그리면 못 그리게 되리
안 불면 못 불게 되리
트럼펫 연주자

Beyond the River

Around this time that day,
Snowflakes blanket the earth and sky.
Without a word between us,
We hold hands tightly.
You and I gaze deeply
into each other's eyes.

In the blink of an eye,
Your look fades, and you are already
On the other side of the river.
Snow obscures my vision,
And I can no longer know
What has become of you there.

A mysterious circuit of reminiscence
has been preserved in your heart,
And you'll be able to live here again.
The wings of imagination are so
  wonderfully attached upon my soul that
I will look ahead of time beyond the river.

강 저편

그날 이맘때도
함박눈이 천지를 덮지
서로 아무 말 없이
손에 손을 굳게 잡지
너와 나는 서로의 눈을
깊이깊이 들여다보리

하염없이 네 모습이
희미해지며 너는 벌써
강 저편에 가 있었지
눈이 온통 저편을 가려
거기서 어찌 되었는지
더는 너의 길 알 수 없지

회상의 오묘한 회로가
네 마음에 간직되었으니
여기를 다시 살게 되리
상상의 날개가 놀랍게
내 영혼에 달렸기에
저편을 미리 넘겨 보리

Reality and Illusion

Ever swaying,
Relentlessly rushing,
What seems real is illusion,
What seems illusion is real.

All, towards the source,
Endlessly running,
The interchange of reality and illusion,
The dispersion and union of energy.

Vanishing and emerging,
The pilgrimage of particles,
Both real and illusory,
They are everywhere and nowhere.

So it seems,
But it is not so,
After one rotation,
It is truly so.

실상과 허상

끊임없이 흔들리며
거침없이 질주하지
실상인 듯 허상이고
허상인 듯 실상이지

모두는 원천을 향해
한없이 달려가는
실상과 허상의 교체
에너지의 분산과 결합이지

사라지고 돋아나는
소립자들의 행각
실상이며 허상이지
어디나 있고 어디도 없지

그렇게 보일 뿐
실은 아니고
한 바퀴 돌면
실로 그렇지

Face to Face

Gazing into each other's eyes,
A signal from someone,
The link has already been established.

What melodies are preserved within
The resonating heartstrings,
Light, wind, and clouds brushing past?

Waves of time and space,
Coming and going between heaven and earth,
Drawing elaborate patterns.

Yesterday, today, and tomorrow,
Facing each other, interlocking fingers,
Uniting here and there.

대면

서로 마주 바라보는 건
누군가의 신호에서리
이미 고리 지어진 거지

빛과 바람과 구름이
스치며 울려간 심금엔
어떤 가락이 간직되지

하늘과 땅 사이 오고 간
시공의 물결이 둘레둘레
정교한 나이테를 그리지

어제와 오늘과 내일이
서로 대면해 깍지를 끼지
여기와 거기를 동여매 가리

제 4 부
캐내는 사람

Part IV
Digger

Stadium

Since I don't know the outcome,
I'll run to the finish line.
Because it is hidden,
I'll run with all my might,
Believing in
Endless possibilities,

Hidden behind the curtain,
It's filled with wonders,
Living in awe.
It's a pity I don't know,
I long to know earnestly,
I'll pour my heart and soul into it.

Those riding the waves,
Those spewing fire,
How joyful they are unable to see ahead.
The day when victory or defeat is declared in advance,
The stadium will be closed,
The kingdom will have no place to stand.

경기장

결과를 모르니
결승선까지
달려 나가리
가려져 있기에
무한의 가능성을 믿고
있는 힘 다해 뛰리

장막 뒤에 있기에
신비가 가득하지
경이 가운데 살리
모르니 안타까워
애타게 알고 싶어
심혈을 기울이지

파도를 타는 이들
불길을 뿜는 것들
앞을 못 보니 기쁘리
승패를 미리 공표하는 날
경기장은 문을 닫게 되리
왕국은 설 자리가 없으리

Passage Rite

Oh, what a wondrous and
Beautiful
Rite of passage.

Donning special attire,
Bearing a unique mission,
One shall pass through here.

Beyond the season of joys and sorrows,
Into the eternal realm,
It is an astonishing path of destiny.

We must depart,
Towards the land of freedom,
We must separate.

Truly poignant, yet
An inexplicable
Beauty it is.

통과의식

실로 경이롭고
아름다운
통과의식이네

특별한 옷을 입고
독특한 임무 띠고
여기를 지나가지

애환의 계절 지나서
영원한 나라에 드는
놀라운 운명의 길이지

자유의 나라 향해
떠나가야 하지
갈라져야 하리

진정 슬프지만
불가사의한
아름다움이지

Digger

What are you so
Passionate about digging?
But you're already digging for spring.

I'm sorry for misunderstanding
That you're doing it just for you.
You dig it up and plant seedlings.

The digger must be
Drawn to something
To do it like that.

In the process of digging,
You might see
The one who planted it.

If you keep going down that path,
You might dig up something
Amazing that you can't even imagine.

캐내는 사람

무엇에 그렇게
열중인가 했더니
벌써 봄을 캐내고 있어

저만 채우는 줄로
오해해서 미안
캐서 모종을 한다네

캐내는 이는 분명
무언가에 끌려
그렇게 하게 되리

캐내는 가운데
모르는 사이
심은 이를 보게 되리

그길로 계속 들어가면
봄뿐이랴 상상 못 할
놀라운 걸 캐내게 되리

Predestined Days

Though each day is already
Predestined,
Each and every day
Will be different and special.

How can last spring
Be the same as this spring?
This autumn will surely
Be different from next autumn.

Though predetermined,
It will never be boring.
Wondrous beauty
Will nurture each day.

What is predestined
Is a fence of protection,
It's the cell membrane of life
That protects eternal life.

Since the path is predestined
And endless,
The boundless dimension
Will dazzlingly unfold.

정해진 나날

나날이 이미
정해져 있지만
매일 매일은
다르고 특별하리

지난봄이 어찌
올봄과 같으랴
올가을은 분명
내년 가을과 다르리

정해졌으나 결코
지루하지 않으리
경이로운 아름다움이
나날을 키워가리

정해져 있는 건
보호의 울타리지
영생을 지켜 주는
생명의 세포막이지

가는 길이 정해진
영원무궁이기에
무궁무진의 차원이
눈부시게 열려오리

Seasonal Light

A figure in a black hat and gray coat
Sits on a riverside bench,
Lost in some contemplation.
The ripples cover the face.

Arms and fingers
Stretched high,
Carried by the waves,
Swaying as a shadow.

The sky is so vast and bright,
As the seasonal light seeps in,
The heavy, rugged coat
Will naturally shed.

Time will bring the moment to discard
The burdens held for far too long.
The weight of solitude will no longer prolong,
As patience guides the soul toward a new song.

계절의 빛

냇가 벤치에 앉은
검은색 모자 회색 외투
무슨 상념에 잠겼는지
잔파도가 얼굴을 덮는다

높이 뻗어 올린
팔과 손가락들
물결에 실려서
그림자로 흔들리지

하늘은 높고 빛나고
계절의 빛이 스며드니
무겁고 투박한 외투는
저절로 벗겨지게 되리

기다리면 때는 오리
홀로 벗어던져 보려고
그처럼 오래 애쓰던걸
시간이 들어와 벗겨주리

The Sound of Knocking

The sound of knocking on the door,
Are you eager to run towards it,
Or do you wish to hide in fear?

Whether you open the window or not,
The astonishing morning light
Will unrelentingly arrive.

The sound calling out to you,
Does it fill you with warm emotion?
Or does it make you tremble with fear?

Whether you listen or not,
The calling will not cease
Until it resonates with you.

두드리는 소리

문을 두드리는 소리
반가워 달려가는지
두려워 숨고 싶은지

창을 열건 않건
놀라운 새벽빛은
어김없이 다가오리

너를 불러대는 소리
뜨거운 감동이 복받치는지
무서워 전신이 떨리는지

네가 듣건 안 듣건
부름은 그침 없으리
너를 울릴 때까지

My Own Time

A bird sits alone on a treetop by the river,
Its head turned towards the distant sky,
But where and what are its eyes staring at?
Perhaps it's taking its own private time.

Does the domain it clicked
Open as expected?
Are information and conversations satisfactory?
Are there any problems due to connection errors?
Is its password constantly being rejected?

Is your own time
Truly your own private time?
It's a time when you're trying to meet someone
Because choices are difficult and frightening,

In the profound stillness
Where all noise is banished,
A time to lend an ear closely
To the subtle whispers
That resonate within the soul.

나만의 시간

냇가 우듬지에 앉은 새
먼 하늘로 머리는 돌렸는데
눈은 어디의 무얼 응시하나
저만의 시간을 갖는 중이리

클릭해 가는 도메인은
기대대로 잘 열려가는지
정보와 대화는 만족스러운지
접속 오류로 문제는 없는지
비밀번호가 자꾸 거부되는지

저만의 시간은 실로
저 혼자만의 시간인지
선택이 어렵고 두려워
누군갈 만나려는 시간이지

안과 밖에서
소음이 제거된
깊은 고요 가운데
영혼에 울려올 미묘한
속삭임에 귀 기울일 시간이지

Disappointment

With great expectations,
They must have entered,
Believing that as they went deeper,
Only beauty would unfold.
They would be shocked to find,
A bed of clutter and filth.

With high ideals in their hearts,
They must have climbed,
Believing that as they climbed higher,
They would reach a celestial realm of wonder,
To live in breathtaking splendor.
They would be sorely disappointed,
By the clash of the monsters' thrones.

It's because you just look at what is seen,
When the unseen is revealed,
Not all is as it seems.
Humans, everywhere still,
Live in the cracks of division.
The chasm between ideals and reality,
Becomes a launching pad for soaring.

실망

큰 기대를 안고
들어왔으리
깊이 들어가면
아름다움만이
펼쳐질 줄로 알았으리
잡동사니 오물이
깔려 있어 놀라리

높은 이상을 품고
올라왔으리
높이 올라만 가면
경탄의 별천지서
기막히게 살 줄 믿었으리
괴물들의 왕좌 다툼에
크게 실망하시리

보이는 것만 보아 그래
안 보이는 걸 보게 되면
다 그런 건 아니리
사람은 어디서나 아직
갈라진 틈 안에서 살지
이상과 현실의 괴리가
비상의 발사대가 되어가리

Entrance and Exit

Metabolism is evidence of life.
Where fire ignites and water flows,
Waste will accumulate there.

Just like eating, drinking, and playing,
We engage in eliminating, spitting, and excreting.
It will become an essential task in life.

As we bring in good materials,
Waste management is crucial,
Life is about controlling the entrance and exit.

When flames overheat,
When waterways clog,
Are measures in place to mitigate?

입구와 출구

신진대사는 삶의 증거
불이 일고 물이 흐르면
거기에는 노폐물이 쌓이리

먹고 마시고 노는 일 못잖게
걷어내고 뱉고 배설해 내야지
삶의 평생 필수작업이 되리

좋은 재료를 들이는 만큼
노폐물 관리가 중요하지
삶은 입구 출구 다스리기

불길이 과열될 때
물길이 막혀갈 때
대책은 강구되었는지

Execution

Knowingly or unwittingly,
Taken and caught,
We would be punished daily.

Don't be a huge disappointment
to the expectant eyes deep inside.
Don't sadden the eyes
looking down from above.

If there were no hands to reach out,
We would have been in jail countless times,
Executed almost daily.

Knowing yet pretending not to know,
Knowing yet acting as if we don't,
Is it because we can't get out?
Or is there another excuse?

Fearing and glancing,
But there's no progress at all,
So, we still have someone to lean on.

처형

알게 또 모르게
찍히고 잡히고
매일 처벌받으리

기대하는 속 눈에
큰 실망 안기지 마시게
내려다보는 눈을
슬프게 하지 마시게

베푸는 손이 없었다면
수도 없이 감옥에 갔으리
거의 매일 처형되었으리

아는 듯 모르는 듯
알아도 모르는 척
헤어나지 못하는지
다른 핑계가 있는지

두려워 눈치 보면서도
아무 진전이 없으니
아직 기댈 데가 있어 서리

Solitary Egret

A solitary egret,
Perhaps left behind,
Perhaps venturing out alone,
Is pecking at the stream.

As the sky rises high,
A cold wind will blow.
Around this time,
They will line up and go somewhere
To take care of tomorrow.

Today's hunger is more
Urgent than anything else.
Tomorrow will take care of tomorrow,
So it will leisurely fill its belly.

해오라기

뒤떨어져서인지
홀로 뛰쳐나왔는지
한 마리 해오라기가
개울물 속을 쪼고 있지

하늘이 드높아지니
찬 바람이 불어오리
이맘때쯤이면
줄지어 어딘가로
내일을 챙기러 갈 때리

오늘의 배고픔이
무엇보다 다급해서지
내일은 내일이 챙길 터니
느긋이 배를 채워가리

제 5 부
가능과 불가능

Part V

Possible and Impossible

Waves

Isn't everything we do
An attempt to live?
Even the most earnest and noble
Decisions to die
Ultimately lead us back to life.

You know that what's yours
Doesn't belong to you.
Since it's not yours
All that you want to do
Won't always work out that way.

It's so hard
And you're exhausted,
But all of this
Are just waves you must overcome
To enter the path of life.

파도

모든 게 살려고
하는 일 아닌지
절실하고 숭고한
죽음의 결단도
결국 다시 살려서지

네가 네 것
아닌 건 알리
네 것이 아니니
네가 하려는 대로
모두 그리 안 되리

너무 힘들어
탈진했어도
이게 모두
살길로 들어가는
넘어야 할 파도이지

Impregnable Fortress

A single passage flies in and
Touches the heartstrings,
Making my steel heart melt.

A single paragraph of words
Pierces the center of my mind,
And the impregnable fortress will fall.

The perspective will shift,
My priorities will change,
I will hold on to the holy grace.

Whose gift is this?
　Amazing ability of the light arrow,
The surging power of rebirth.

철옹성

한 악절이 날아 들어와
심금을 퉁기니
강철 심장이 녹아나지

한 단락 말 화살이
마음 중심에 박히니
철옹성이 무너지리

시각이 달라져 가리
우선순위가 뒤바뀌리
거룩한 은혜를 붙잡으리

누가 보내준 선물이지
놀라운 빛 화살의 능력
솟아오르는 소생의 힘

Wind and Door

The path of the wind is impermanent,
Never knowing where or when it will bend.
The cries of migrating birds
Echo through the cloud-covered skies.

Unseen and untouchable,
We assume it's nonexistent, lost in confusion.
Don't rush to close the door,
For it was meant to be open from the start.

The wind will blow,
To open the door?
or will it close it,
Enforce it or snatch it away?

Where and when
Will your door faces,
Is it a place to crawl into?
Or a day to soar up high?

바람과 문

바람의 길은 무상하니
언제 어디로 길을 잡을지
철새들의 울부짖음이
구름 덮인 하늘에 맴돌지

안 보이니 안 잡히니
없는 줄 알고 당황하리
미리 문을 닫지 마시게
본시 열라고 낸 문이리

바람이 불어오리
문을 열어줄 건지
닫아 버릴 건지
보태줄지 빼앗을지

어디 어느 때로
너의 문은 향해 있지
기어들어 갈 곳인지
솟구쳐 오를 날인지

Yoga Walk

Arms and hands, bending and stretching,
In rhythm with the steps,
Refining breath and heartbeat,
Striding down the walking path.

Whether pulling or releasing,
The movements of arms and legs
Engage in a constant dialogue
With the neural network,
Reaching up in supplication,
Bringing down and holding close.

Yoga walk along the riverbank,
A celestial excursion.
Where have you reached now?
Whom are you meeting?

요가 산책

팔과 손 굽혀펴기를
발장단에 맞춰가며
호흡과 박동을 가다듬어
산책길을 활보하는 이

잡아당기려는지
놓아버리려는지
팔다리 손 움직임이
계속 뇌 망과 교신하리
들어 올려 간구하며
내려받아 간직하리

강변로 요가 산책이
하늘 나들이 삼매경이지
지금 어디쯤 닿아있지
누구를 만나고 있는지

Warning Signs

When the flames of devotion
Are burning brightly,
If something goes wrong,
Subject and object will be reversed.

Something is not going well,
Sighs come out frequently,
The mind becomes stuffy.
If overheating continues,
Things will turn hazy before the eyes.
These are the warning signs
Of a derailment crisis

The sound of the whip of reproach,
Echoing from the inner mirror,
Shakes the network of consciousness,
And delivers warning signs.

경고신호

헌신의 불길이
한창 타오를 때
자칫 잘못되면
주객이 전도되리

무언가 잘 안 풀리며
한숨이 자주 나오리
마음이 답답해지리
과열이 더 지속되면
눈앞이 아뜩해지리
전도의 위기를 알리는
탈선 경고신호이지

속 거울에서 울려오는
책망의 채찍 소리가
의식 망을 격동하여
넘겨주는 경고징후이지

Possible and Impossible

Daring to attempt the impossible,
Is it due to ignorance
and arrogance?
How could heaven allow
so much effort to be
poured out in vain?

Possibility and impossibility
Are functions of time and space.
Are you trying to adjust your time
To the heaven's time?
Or set the heaven's time
To your time?

Is it a process of training
To awaken and broaden
Your perspective?
It's been hinted and
Explained for so long,
But you still don't understand.

가능과 불가능

불가능할 줄도 모르고
당돌히 시도하는 건
우매와 만용의 소치인지
하늘은 어찌 헛되이
그처럼 심혈을 토하도록
내버려 두는 것인지

가능과 불가능은
시공의 함수이지
하늘 시간에 네 시간을
맞추려나
네 시간에 하늘 시간을
맞추려느냐

일깨워 주려는
시각을 넓혀주려는
단련의 과정인지
귀띔해 주었는데
일러준 지 오랜데
못 알아챘으리

Empty House

In a day when nature's beauty unfolds,
Why does your countenance seem so cold?
Surely, a burden weighs on your mind.

Joy, shadowed by doubt's lingering haze,
Life, driven by the will to survive,
Peace, lost in the battles we strive.

Being pushed means giving up,
By exposing our vulnerabilities,
Allowing a gap in our territory.

Unable to welcome friendly forces,
The void that's created will soon be swayed,
Occupied by the formidable enemy.

A house devoid of light's embrace,
Where only cobwebs and dust find space,
A place where joy's blossoms can't accrue.

빈집

잎과 꽃이 피는 날인데
왜 표정이 착잡하지
사유가 분명히 있으리

불확실에 밀린 기쁨
생존에 밀린 생활
싸움에 밀린 평화

밀리는 건 내주는 일
허점을 드러내서
영역을 허용한 거리

우군을 맞아들이지 못해
생겨난 빈 곳이 가공할
적군에게 점령당했으리

빛이 못 든 빈집이지
거미줄과 먼지뿐이니
기쁨의 꽃이 못 피리

Bystander

Living in this world
There are three kinds of people
Believers
Rebels
Bystanders

Not enough
to believe
Too overwhelmed
to rebel
Becoming a bystander

Even at the crossroads
Of life and death
Trapped within reason
Unable to make a decision
Remaining a bystander

Did you reject the outstretched hand?
Did you hesitate and fail to see?
You still remain a bystander
It's a hurdle race
That cannot be overcome alone
Without someone to lead

방관자

세상에 사는
세 부류 사람
신봉자
반역자
방관자

신봉하기엔
아직 모자라고
반역하려니
너무나 벅차
방관자가 되리

삶과 죽음의
갈림길에서도
이성 안에 갇혀
결단을 못 내린 채
방관자로 남으려나

내민 손을 뿌리쳤는지
주저하느라 못 보았는지
아직도 방관자로 남아있지
이끄는 이 없이 혼자서는
못 넘는 장애물경주이지

Spring Vibes

To embrace the spring vibes,
Putting everything aside,
All gather together,
People and birds,
Trees and streams.

Someone must have told them,
Whispered something to them,
They quietly receive
The baptism of cascading photons,
And will deeply recharge the spring energy.

Beneath the sun's luminous gaze,
Their hidden eyes will open,
Their imprisoned hearts will bloom,
They will yearn to soar through the sky,
And stand tall to embrace freedom.

Wherever the spring light touches,
Life emerges, vibrant and new,
Hopes will bloom,
It's a celebration of planets
Orbiting around the sun.

봄기운

봄기운을 받으려
모든 걸 제쳐 놓고
모두 모여들지
사람도 새도
나무도 냇물도

누군가 알려주었으리
무언가로 귀띔하였으리
쏟아져 내리는 광자의
세례를 다소곳이 받는다
봄기운을 깊이 충전하리

눈부신 빛살 가운데
가려졌던 눈이 트이리
갇혔던 마음이 피어나리
창공을 날고 싶어지리
자유를 만끽하려 서지

봄빛이 닿는 데마다
생명이 돌아나오리
소망이 피어오르리
태양을 공전하는
행성들의 축제이네

Flames

As flames rise high,
Illuminating the path ahead,
I run without hesitation.

The fire ignites,
My eyes open,
Wings sprout from my back.

Determination takes hold,
Hesitation fades away,
I soar into the heavens.

Sparks fly,
Wings spread wide,
I embrace freedom.

The flames surge,
Amid the dazzling light,
I become the wings of liberty.

불꽃

불꽃이 오르며
비춰주는 길로
거침없이 달리지

불길이 일어나니
눈이 열리며
날개가 달리지

결단이 내려지리
두렴이 사라지리
창공을 날아오르지

불꽃이 튀며
날개가 펼쳐지지
자유를 만끽하리

불길이 솟으며
놀라운 빛 가운데
자유의 날개가 되지

Buds

On a day when the wind changes direction,
Setting a course for the southeast,
The sky will be dazzling,
And the forest will be wonderfully still.

Soon, the sound of departure
Will echo through the mountains and rivers.
Magnolia, forsythia,
Azalea, and cherries,
Following the signal, will open their flower buds,

What preparation is there?
Time has already arranged it all,
Gathering together what is not yet complete,
It will lift it up and make it bloom.

Willows with their tops cut off
Embrace the spring light in the midst of trials,
Pitiful reeds by the stream
Are staring at something in the wind,
Soon, buds will sprout.

새싹

바람이 방향을 돌려
동남으로 길을 잡는 날
하늘은 눈부시고
숲은 놀랍게 고요하리

이제 곧 출발 탄이
강산에 울려 퍼지리
목련도 개나리도
진달래도 벚찌도
신호 따라 꽃눈을 트리

준비가 따로 있으랴
시간이 모두 마련해주지
미달한 것도 함께 잡아
끌어올려 피어 내주리

우듬지 잘린 수양버들
시련 가운데 봄빛을 품지
가여운 냇가 갈대꽃들
바람 속에 뭔갈 응시하지
곧 새싹이 돌아 오르리

| Epilogue |

Perspective

It seems like it can be seen clearly
If we look close,
But it won't be visible any better.

If we fall into it,
Our eyes will be blinded,
It's so invisible that
We can't tell what it is.

Wonderful and beautiful things
Can only be seen
in their entirety
By applying a given perspective.

Not just the wonders of the universe,
But the mysteries of the beginning,
And the other side of eternity as well.

| 에필로그 |

원근법

가까이서 보면
잘 보일 것 같으나
더 잘 안 보이리

그 안에 빠지면
눈이 가리니
아주 안 보이리
무언지 알 수 없으리

경이롭고 아름다운 건
주어진 원근법을
제대로 적용해야지
전체를 보게 되리

우주의 불가사의뿐이랴
태초의 신비가 그렇고
영원의 저쪽도 그렇지

About the Author

Lee Won-Ro

Poet as well as medical doctor (cardiologist), professor, chancellor of hospitals and university president, Lee Won-Ro`s career has been prominent in his brilliant literary activities along with his extensive experiences and contributions in medical science and practice.

Lee Won-Ro is the author of fifty five poetry books along with thirteene anthologies. He also published extensively including ten books related to medicine both for professionals and general readership.

Lee Won-Ro`s poetic world pursues the fundamental themes with profound aesthetic enthusiasm. His work combines wisdom and knowledge derived from his scientific background with his artistic power stemming from creative imagination and astute intuition.

Lee Won-Ro`s verse embroiders refined tints and serene tones on the fabric of embellished words.

Poet Lee Won-Ro explores the universe in conjunction with

his expertise in intellectual, affective and spiritual domains as a specialist in medicine and science to create his unique artistic world.

This book along with "On the Road", "Winter Gift", "Fair Winds", "Spiral Staircase", "The Watershed", "The Seed of Eternity", "Milky Way In DNA", "Signs of Recovery", "Applause", "Invitation", "Night Sky", "Revival", "The Promise", "Time Capsule", "The Tea Cup and the Sea", "The Tunnel of Waves", "The Tomorrow within Today", "Our Home", "The Sound of the Wind", "Flowers and Stars", "Corona Panic", "Chorus", "Waves", "Thanks and Empathy", "Red Berries", "Dialogue", "A Mural of Sounds", "Focal Point", "Day Break", "Prelude to a Pilgrimage", "Rehearsal", "TimeLapse Panorama", "Eve Celebration", "A Trumpet Call", "Right on Cue", "Why Do You Push My Back", "Space Walk", "Phoenix Parade", "The Vortex of Dances", "Pearling", "Priming Water", "A Glint of Light", "The River Unstoppable", "Song of Stars", "The Land of Floral Buds", "A Flute Player", "The Glow of a Firefly", "Resonance", "Wrinkles in Time", "Wedding Day", "Synapse", "Miracles are Everywhere", "Unity in Variety" and "Signal Hunter" are available at Amazon.com/author/leewonro or kdp.amazon.com/bookshelf(paperbacks and e-books).

글쓴이

이원로

　시인이자 의사(심장전문의), 교수, 명예의료원장, 전 대학교총장인 이원로 시인은 월간문학으로 등단, "빛과 소리를 넘어서", "햇빛 유난한 날에", "청진기와 망원경", "팬터마임", "피아니시모", "모자이크", "순간의 창", "바람의 지도", "우주의 배꼽", "시집가는 날", "시냅스", "기적은 어디에나", "화이부동", "신호추적자", "시간의 주름", "울림", "반딧불", "피리 부는 사람", "꽃눈 나라", "별들의 노래", "멈출 수 없는 강물", "섬광", "마중물", "진주잡이", "춤의 소용돌이", "우주유영", "어찌 등을 미시나요", "불사조 행렬", "마침 좋은 때에", "나팔소리", "전야제", "타임랩스 파노라마", "장도의 서막", "새벽", "초점", "소리 벽화", "물결", "감사와 공감", "합창", "코로나 공황", "대화", "빨간 열매", "꽃과 별", "바람 소리", "우리집", "오늘 안의 내일", "파도의 터널", "찻잔과 바다", "타임캡슐", "약속", "소생", "밤하늘", "초대장", "박수갈채", "회복의 눈빛", "DNA 안 은하수", "영원의 씨", "분수령", "나선계단", "순풍", "겨울 선물", "길 위에서", "카운트다운" 등 55권의 시집과 13권의 시선집을 출간했다. 시집 외에도 그는 전공 분야의 교과서와 의학 정보를 일반인들에게 쉽게 전달하기 위한 실용서를 여러 권 집필했다.

이원로 시인의 시 세계에는 생명의 근원적 주제에 대한 탐색이 담겨져 있다. 그의 작품은 과학과 의학에서 유래된 지혜와 지식을 배경으로 기민한 통찰력과 상상력을 동원하여 진실하고 아름답고 영원한 우주를 추구하고 있다. 그의 시는 순화된 색조와 우아한 운율의 언어로 예술적 동경을 수놓아간다.

이원로 시인은 과학과 의학 전문가로서의 지성적, 감성적, 영적 경험을 바탕으로 그의 독특한 예술 세계를 개척해가고 있다.

이 시집을 비롯하여 "길 위에서", "겨울 선물", "순풍", "나선계단", "분수령", "영원의 씨", "DNA 안 은하수", "회복의 눈빛", "초대장", "밤하늘", "소생", "약속", "타임캡슐", "찻잔과 바다", "파도의 터널", "오늘 안의 내일", "우리집", "바람 소리", "꽃과 별", "빨간 열매", "대화", "코로나 공황", "합창", "물결", "감사와 공감", "소리 벽화", "초점", "새벽", "장도의 서막", "타임랩스 파노라마", "전야제", "나팔소리", "마침 좋은 때에", "어찌 등을 미시나요", "우주유영", "불사조 행렬", "춤의 소용돌이", "진주잡이", "마중물", "섬광", "멈출 수 없는 강물", "별들의 노래", "꽃눈 나라", "피리 부는 사람", "반딧불", "울림", "시집가는 날", "시냅스", "기적은 어디에나", "화이부동", "신호추적자", "시간의 주름" 등은 아래에서 구입할 수 있다.

Amazon.com/author/leewonro와 kdp.amazon.com/bookshelf(paperbacks and e-books)

카운트다운
Countdown

2024년 11월 5일 인쇄
2024년 11월 15일 발행

지은이 / 이원로
발행인 / 박진환
펴낸곳 / 조선문학사
등록번호 / 1-2733
주소 / 03730 서울 서대문구 통일로 389(홍제동)
대표전화 / 02-730-2255
팩스 / 02-723-9373
E-mail / chosunmh2@daum.net

ISBN 979-11-6354-322-0

정가 10,000원

* 인지는 저자와 합의 하에 생략
* 잘못된 책은 서점에서 교환해 드립니다.